Impressum
Verlag: BABADADA GmbH, Nedderfeld 112 , 22529 Hamburg
Geschäftsführer / Verlagsleitung: Harald Hof
Druck: Books on Demand GmbH, In de Tarpen 42, 22848 Norderstedt

Imprint
Publisher: BABADADA GmbH, Nedderfeld 112 , 22529 Hamburg, Germany
Managing Director / Publishing direction: Harald Hof
Print: Books on Demand GmbH, In de Tarpen 42, 22848 Norderstedt

教室
classroom

除
divide

186/2

黑板
board

校園
school yard

老師
teacher

紙
paper

書寫
write

筆
pen

辦公桌
desk

直尺
ruler

書
book

學生
pupil

書包
satchel

鉛筆盒
pencil case

鉛筆
pencil

削鉛筆機
pencil sharpener

橡皮擦
rubber

畫板
drawing pad

圖畫
drawing

畫筆
paintbrush

顏料盒
paint box

剪刀
scissors

膠水
glue

練習冊
exercise book

家庭作業
homework

12

數字
number

2+2

加
add

5-2

減
subtract

2×2

乘
multiply

計算
calculate

A

字母
letter

ABCDEFG HIJKLMN OPQRSTU VWXYZ

字母表
alphabet

hello

字
word

課文
text

讀
read

粉筆
chalk

上課
lesson

登記
register

考試
exam

證書
certificate

校服
school uniform

教育
education

百科全書
encyclopedia

大學
university

顯微鏡
microscope

地圖
map

廢紙簍
paper bin

飯店
hotel

青年旅社
hostel

外幣兌換處
bureau de change

手提箱
suitcase

汽車
car

語言
language

是/否
yes / no

好的
Okay

您好
hello

翻譯人員
translator

謝謝
Thank you

……多少錢？

how much does ... cost?

我不明白

I do not understand

問題

problem

晚上好！

Good evening!

早上好！

Good morning!

晚安！

Good night!

再見

bye bye

方向

direction

行李

luggage

包

bag

背包

backpack

客人

guest

房間

room

睡袋

sleeping bag

帳篷

tent

旅行資訊

tourist information

海灘

beach

信用卡

credit card

早餐

breakfast

午餐

lunch

晚餐

dinner

票

ticket

電梯

lift

郵票

stamp

邊界

border

海關

customs

大使館

embassy

簽證

visa

護照

passport

飛機
aeroplane

船
ship

消防車
fire engine

公車
bus

卡車
truck

汽艇
motorboat

汽車
car

腳踏車
bike

渡輪

ferry

小船

boat

機車

motorbike

警車

police car

賽車

racing car

租車

rental car

拼車
....
car sharing

拖車
....
breakdown truck

垃圾車
....
refuse truck

馬達
....
motor

汽油
....
fuel

加油站
....
petrol station

交通標識
....
traffic sign

交通
....
traffic

交通堵塞
....
traffic jam

停車場
....
car park

火車站
....
train station

軌道
....
tracks

火車
....
train

路面電車
....
tram

客車廂
....
carriage

直升機

helicopter

機場

airport

塔

tower

乘客

passenger

集裝箱

container

紙板箱

carton

手推車

cart

籃子

basket

起飛/降落

take off / land

城市

city

村莊

village

市中心

city centre

房子

house

電影院
cinema

廣告
advert

路燈
street light

街道
street

計程車
taxi

小吃店
snack shop

行人
pedestrian

人行道
pavement

斑馬線
zebra crossing

垃圾箱
bin

十字路口
crossing

紅綠燈
traffic lights

小屋

hut

公寓

flat

火車站

train station

市政廳

town hall

博物館

museum

學校

school

城市 - city

大學
university

銀行
bank

醫院
hospital

飯店
hotel

藥房
pharmacy

辦公室
office

書店
book shop

商店
shop

花店
florist's

超市
supermarket

市場
market

百貨商店
department store

魚店
fishmonger's

購物中心
shopping centre

海港
harbour

公園
park

長凳
bench

橋
bridge

樓梯
stairs

捷運
underground

隧道
tunnel

公車站
bus stop

酒吧
bar

餐館
restaurant

郵筒
postbox

路標
road sign

停車計時器
parking meter

動物園
zoo

游泳池
swimming pool

清真寺
mosque

農場
farm

污染
pollution

墓地
graveyard

教堂
church

操場
playground

寺廟
temple

地形
landscape

樹葉
leaf

指示牌
signpost

路
way

草地
meadow

石頭
stone

徒步旅行
者
hiker

樹
tree

河
river

草
grass

花
flower

峽谷
valley

丘陵
hill

湖
lake

森林
forest

沙漠
desert

火山
volcano

城堡
castle

彩虹
rainbow

蘑菇
mushroom

棕櫚樹
palm tree

蚊子
mosquito

蒼蠅
fly

螞蟻
ant

蜜蜂
bee

蜘蛛
spider

地形 - landscape

甲蟲

beetle

青蛙

frog

松鼠

squirrel

刺蝟

hedgehog

野兔

hare

貓頭鷹

owl

鳥

bird

天鵝

swan

野豬

boar

鹿

deer

麋鹿

moose

水壩

dam

風力發電機

wind turbine

太陽能電池板

solar panel

氣候

climate

服務生
waiter

菜譜
menu

椅子
chair

披薩餅
pizza

湯
soup

桌布
tablecloth

餐具
cutlery

前菜
starter

主菜
main course

甜點
dessert

飲料
drinks

食物
food

瓶子
bottle

速食
fast food

街邊小吃
street food

茶壺
teapot

糖盒
sugar bowl

一份飯菜
portion

義式咖啡機
espresso machine

高腳椅
high chair

帳單
bill

托盤
tray

刀
knife

餐叉
fork

勺子
spoon

茶匙
teaspoon

餐巾
serviette

玻璃杯
glass

碟子
plate

湯盤
soup plate

碟子
saucer

醬
sauce

鹽瓶
salt cellar

胡椒研磨罐
pepper mill

醋
vinegar

食用油
oil

調味料
spices

番茄醬
ketchup

芥末
mustard

美乃滋
mayonnaise

特價
special offer

顧客
customer

乳製品
dairy

水果
fruit

購物車
trolley

FOR

肉鋪

butcher´s

麵包店

baker´s

稱重

weigh

蔬菜

vegetables

肉

meat

冷凍食品

frozen food

冷盤
cold meat

罐頭食品
tinned food

洗衣粉
washing powder

甜食
sweets

日用品
household products

清潔用品
cleaning products

銷售員
salesperson

收銀機
till

收銀員
cashier

購物清單
shopping list

開放時間
opening hours

錢包
wallet

信用卡
credit card

袋子
bag

塑膠袋
plastic bag

水
water

果汁
juice

牛奶
milk

可樂
coke

紅酒
wine

啤酒
beer

酒
alcohol

可可
cocoa

茶
tea

咖啡
coffee

義式濃縮咖啡
espresso

卡布奇諾
cappuccino

香蕉

banana

蘋果

apple

柳丁

orange

西瓜

melon

檸檬

lemon

胡蘿蔔

carrot

大蒜

garlic

竹子

bamboo

洋蔥

onion

蘑菇

mushroom

堅果

nuts

麵條

noodles

義大利麵

spaghetti

米飯

rice

沙拉

salad

薯條

chips

炸馬鈴薯

fried potatoes

披薩餅

pizza

漢堡

hamburger

三明治

sandwich

炸豬排

cutlet

火腿

ham

義大利臘腸

salami

香腸

sausage

雞肉

chicken

烤肉

roast

魚

fish

燕麥片

porridge oats

木斯里

muesli

玉米片

cornflakes

麵粉

flour

牛角麵包

croissant

麵包捲

bread roll

麵包

bread

吐司

toast

餅乾

biscuits

奶油

butter

凝乳

curd

蛋糕

cake

蛋

egg

煎蛋

fried egg

起司

cheese

冰淇淋

ice cream

糖

sugar

蜂蜜

honey

果醬

jam

巧克力醬

chocolate spread

咖哩

curry

農舍
farmhouse

糧倉
barn

稻草捆
straw bale

田野
field

馬
horse

拖車
trailer

馬駒
foal

拖拉機
tractor

驢
donkey

羔羊
lamb

羊
sheep

山羊
goat

奶牛
cow

小牛
calf

豬
pig

小豬
piglet

公牛
bull

鵝

goose

鴨

duck

小雞

chick

母雞

hen

公雞

cock

鼠

rat

貓

cat

老鼠

mouse

牛

ox

狗

dog

狗屋

doghouse

花園澆水軟管

garden hose

澆水壺

watering can

長柄大鐮刀

scythe

犁

plough

鐮刀
sickle

鋤頭
hoe

長柄草耙
pitchfork

斧頭
axe

獨輪手推車
wheelbarrow

飼料槽
trough

牛奶罐
milk can

麻布袋
sack

柵欄
fence

馬廄
stable

溫室
greenhouse

土壤
soil

種子
seed

肥料
fertilizer

聯合收割機
combine harvester

收割

harvest

收割

harvest

地瓜

yams

小麥

wheat

大豆

soy

土豆

potato

玉米

corn

油菜籽

rapeseed

果樹

fruit tree

樹薯

cassava

穀物

cereals

煙囪
chimney

屋頂
roof

落水管
drain pipe

窗戶
window

車庫
garage

門鈴
doorbell

門
door

垃圾桶
rubbish bin

信箱
letterbox

花園
garden

客廳
living room

浴室
bathroom

廚房
kitchen

臥室
bedroom

兒童房
child's room

餐廳
dining room

地板

floor

牆壁

wall

天花板

ceiling

地窖

cellar

三溫暖

sauna

陽臺

balcony

露臺

terrace

游泳池

pool

割草機

lawn mower

被單

sheet

床罩

bedspread

床

bed

掃帚

broom

水桶

bucket

開關

switch

壁紙
wallpaper

相片
picture

擱架
shelf

櫃燈
lamp

櫥櫃
cupboard

電視
television

壁爐
fireplace

花
flower

墊子
cushion

沙發
sofa

花瓶
vase

遙控器
remote control

地毯

carpet

窗簾

curtain

餐桌

table

椅子

chair

搖椅

rocking chair

扶手椅

armchair

書

book

毯子

blanket

裝飾品

decoration

木柴

firewood

電影

film

高傳真音響

hi-fi equipment

鑰匙

key

報紙

newspaper

油畫

painting

海報

poster

收音機

radio

筆記本

notepad

吸塵器

hoover

仙人掌

cactus

蠟燭

candle

冰箱
fridge

微波爐
microwave oven

廚房秤
kitchen scales

洗潔精
detergent

烤麵包機
toaster

烤箱
oven

冰櫃
freezer

垃圾桶
rubbish bin

洗碗機
dishwasher

炊具

cooker

鍋

pot

鑄鐵鍋

cast-iron pot

炒鍋

wok / kadai

平底鍋

pan

水壺

kettle

蒸鍋

steamer

烤盤

baking tray

陶瓷鍋

crockery

馬克杯

mug

碗

bowl

筷子

chopsticks

長柄勺

ladle

鏟子

spatula

攪拌器

whisk

濾網

strainer

篩子

sieve

磨碎機

grater

研缽

mortar

燒烤

barbecue

明火

open fire

菜板
chopping board

擀麵杖
rolling pin

開瓶器
corkscrew

罐子
can

開罐器
can opener

隔熱手套
pot holder

水槽
sink

刷子
brush

海綿
sponge

攪拌機
blender

冷藏箱
deep freezer

奶瓶
baby bottle

水龍頭
tap

供暖裝置
heating

淋浴
shower

毛巾
towel

浴簾
shower curtain

泡沫浴
bubble bath

浴缸
bathtub

玻璃杯
glass

洗衣機
washing machine

瓷磚
tiles

水龍頭
tap

便壺
potty

水槽
sink

廁所

toilet

蹲便器

squat toilet

坐浴器

bidet

小便斗

urinal

廁紙

toilet paper

馬桶刷

toilet brush

牙刷
toothbrush

牙膏
toothpaste

牙線
dental floss

洗
wash

手持式蓮蓬頭
handheld shower

沖洗器
douche

洗臉盆
basin

洗背刷
back brush

肥皂
soap

沐浴露
shower gel

洗髮乳
shampoo

法蘭絨
flannel

排水
drain

乳霜
cream

除臭劑
deodorant

鏡子

mirror

手鏡

hand mirror

刮鬍刀

razor

刮鬍泡沫

shaving foam

鬍後水

aftershave

梳子

comb

刷子

brush

吹風機

hair dryer

噴髮定型劑

hairspray

化妝品

makeup

唇膏

lipstick

指甲油

nail varnish

化妝棉

cotton wool

指甲剪

nail scissors

香水

perfume

洗漱包
washbag

凳子
stool

計重秤
weighing scale

浴袍
bathrobe

橡膠手套
rubber gloves

衛生棉條
tampon

衛生棉
sanitary towel

化學廁所
chemical toilet

鬧鐘
alarm clock

毛絨玩具
cuddly toy

玩具車
toy car

撥浪鼓
rattle

玩具屋
doll's house

禮物
present

氣球
balloon

床
bed

嬰兒車
pram

撲克牌
deck of cards

拼圖
jigsaw

漫畫
comic

樂高積木
lego bricks

積木玩具
building blocks

公仔
action figure

嬰兒服
romper suit

飛盤
Frisbee

床鈴玩具
mobile

棋盤遊戲
board game

骰子
dice

火車模型
model train set

安撫奶嘴
dummy

派對
party

繪本
picture book

球
ball

洋娃娃
doll

玩
play

沙坑

sandpit

鞦韆

swing

玩具

toys

電玩遊戲

video game console

三輪車

tricycle

泰迪熊

teddy bear

衣櫃

wardrobe

衣服
clothing

襪子

socks

長襪

stockings

緊身褲

tights

圍巾
scarf

雨傘
umbrella

皮帶
belt

T恤
t-shirt

靴子
boots

拖鞋
slippers

運動鞋
trainers

涼鞋
sandals

鞋
shoes

雨靴
rubber boots

內褲
underpants

胸罩
bra

背心
vest

衣服 - clothing

身體
body

褲子
trousers

牛仔褲
jeans

短裙
skirt

女式襯衫
blouse

襯衫
shirt

套頭衫
pullover

連帽上衣
hoodie

西裝夾克
blazer

夾克
jacket

外套
coat

雨衣
raincoat

套裝
costume

連衣裙
dress

婚紗
wedding dress

西裝
suit

睡袍
nightgown

睡衣
pyjamas

莎麗
sari

頭巾
headscarf

包頭巾
turban

波卡
burqa

卡夫坦
kaftan

(阿拉伯式)長袍
abaya

泳衣
swimsuit

男式泳褲
trunks

短褲
shorts

運動服
tracksuit

圍裙
apron

手套
gloves

衣服 - clothing

鈕扣
button

眼鏡
glasses

手鏈
bracelet

項鍊
necklace

戒指
ring

耳環
earring

便帽
cap

衣架
coat hanger

帽子
hat

領帶
tie

拉鍊
zipper

安全帽
helmet

背帶
braces

校服
school uniform

制服
uniform

圍兜
bib

安撫奶嘴
dummy

尿布
nappy

辦公室
office

伺服器
server

檔案櫃
filing cabinet

印表機
printer

螢幕
monitor

紙
paper

滑鼠
mouse

辦公桌
desk

資料夾
folder

鍵盤
keyboard

廢紙簍
paper bin

椅子
chair

電腦
computer

咖啡杯
coffee mug

計算機
calculator

網際網路
internet

筆記型電腦
laptop

信件
letter

簡訊
message

行動電話
mobile

網路
network

影印機
photocopier

軟體
software

電話
telephone

插座
plug socket

傳真機
fax machine

表格
form

檔案
document

買

buy

付錢

pay

交易

trade

現金

money

美元

dollar

歐元

euro

日元

yen

盧布

rouble

瑞士法郎

Swiss franc

人民幣

renminbi yuan

盧比

rupee

提款處

cashpoint

外幣兌換處

bureau de change

金

gold

銀

silver

石油

oil

能源

energy

價格

price

合約

contract

稅金

tax

股票

stock

工作

work

職員

employee

老闆

employer

工廠

factory

商店

shop

經濟 - economy

警官
police officer

消防員
fireman

廚師
cook

醫師
doctor

飛行員
pilot

園丁

gardener

木匠

carpenter

裁縫

seamstress

法官

judge

化學家

chemist

演員

actor

公車司機

bus driver

計程車司機

taxi driver

漁夫

fisherman

清洗女工

cleaning lady

屋頂工

roofer

服務生

waiter

獵人

hunter

畫家

painter

麵包師

baker

電工

electrician

建築工人

builder

工程師

engineer

屠夫

butcher

水管工

plumber

郵差

postman

士兵

soldier

建築師

architect

收銀員

cashier

花農

florist

理髮師

hairdresser

售票員

conductor

機械技師

mechanic

船長

captain

牙醫

dentist

科學家

scientist

拉比

rabbi

伊瑪目

imam

和尚

monk

牧師

clergyman

鐵錘
hammer

螺絲起子
screwdriver

鉗子
pliers

扳手
spanner

手電筒
torch

挖掘機

digger

工具箱

toolbox

梯子

ladder

鋸子

saw

釘子

nails

鑽機

drill

修
repair

鏟子
shovel

糟糕！
Damn!

畚箕
dustpan

油漆桶
paint pot

螺絲
screws

樂器
musical instruments

打擊樂器
drum kit

揚聲器
loudspeaker

吉他
guitar

低音提琴
double bass

小號
trumpet

鋼琴
piano

小提琴
violin

貝斯
bass

定音鼓
timpani

鼓
drums

電子琴
keyboard

薩克斯風
saxophone

長笛
flute

麥克風
microphone

入口
entrance

老虎
tiger

籠子
cage

斑馬
zebra

動物飼料
animal feed

熊貓
panda

動物

animals

大象

elephant

袋鼠

kangaroo

犀牛

rhino

大猩猩

gorilla

熊

bear

駱駝

camel

鴕鳥

ostrich

獅子

lion

猴子

monkey

紅鶴

flamingo

鸚鵡

parrot

北極熊

polar bear

企鵝

penguin

鯊魚

shark

孔雀

peacock

蛇

snake

鱷魚

crocodile

動物園管理員

zookeeper

海豹

seal

美洲豹

jaguar

矮種馬

pony

豹

leopard

河馬

hippo

長頸鹿

giraffe

老鷹

eagle

野豬

boar

魚

fish

龜

turtle

海象

walrus

狐狸

fox

羚羊

gazelle

橄欖球
American football

騎腳踏車
cycling

網球
tennis

籃球
basketball

游泳
swimming

拳擊
boxing

冰球
ice hockey

美式足球
football

羽毛球
badminton

田徑
athletics

手球
handball

滑雪
skiing

馬球
polo

笑 laugh

跳 jump

擁抱 hug

走路 walk

唱 sing

做夢 dream

祈禱 pray

親吻 kiss

書寫
write

畫
draw

展示
show

推
push

給
give

拿
take

有
have

做
do

當
be

站
stand

跑
run

拉
pull

丟
throw

摔倒
fall

躺
lie

等待
wait

攜帶
carry

坐
sit

穿衣
get dressed

睡覺
sleep

醒來
wake up

看
look at

哭
cry

擊
stroke

梳頭
comb

交談
talk

明白
understand

問
ask

聽
listen

喝
drink

吃
eat

清理
tidy up

愛
love

做飯
cook

開車
drive

飛
fly

航行

sail

計算

calculate

讀

read

學習

learn

工作

work

結婚

marry

縫

sew

刷牙

brush teeth

殺

kill

抽菸

smoke

寄

send

祖母
grandmother

祖父
grandfather

父親
father

母親
mother

嬰兒
baby

女兒
daughter

兒子
son

客人
guest

阿姨
aunt

叔叔
uncle

兄弟
brother

姐妹
sister

前額
forehead

眼睛
eye

肩膀
shoulder

手指
finger

臉
face

下巴
chin

手
hand

乳房
breast

腿
leg

手臂
arm

嬰兒

baby

男人

man

女人

woman

女孩

girl

男孩

boy

頭

head

背部

back

肚子

belly

肚臍

belly button

腳趾

toe

腳後跟

heel

骨頭

bone

臀部

hip

膝蓋

knee

手肘

elbow

鼻子

nose

屁股

bottom

皮膚

skin

臉頰

cheek

耳朵

ear

嘴唇

lip

嘴
mouth

牙齒
tooth

舌頭
tongue

腦
brain

心臟
heart

肌肉
muscle

肺
lung

肝臟
liver

胃
stomach

腎臟
kidneys

性交
sex

保險套
condom

卵子
ovum

精子
semen

懷孕
pregnancy

月事

menstruation

陰道

vagina

陰莖

penis

眉毛

eyebrow

頭髮

hair

脖子

neck

醫院
hospital

急救車
ambulance

輪椅
wheelchair

骨折
fracture

醫師
doctor

急診室
emergency room

護理師
nurse

緊急情形
emergency

昏迷
unconscious

痛
pain

受傷
injury

出血
bleeding

心臟病發作
heart attack

中風
stroke

過敏
allergy

咳嗽
cough

發燒
fever

流感
flu

腹瀉
diarrhoea

頭痛
headache

癌症
cancer

糖尿病
diabetes

外科醫師
surgeon

手術刀
scalpel

手術
operation

醫院 - hospital

電腦斷層掃描
CT

X光
x-ray

超音波
ultrasound

口罩
face mask

疾病
disease

候診室
waiting room

拐杖
crutch

石膏
plaster

繃帶
bandage

注射
injection

聽診器
stethoscope

擔架
stretcher

體溫計
clinical thermometer

出生
birth

超重
overweight

助聽器
hearing aid

消毒液
disinfectant

感染
infection

病毒
virus

愛滋病
HIV / AIDS

藥物
medicine

接種疫苗
vaccination

藥片
tablets

藥丸
pill

急救電話
emergency call

血壓計
blood pressure monitor

生病/健康
sick / healthy

救命！

Help!

突擊

assault

警報

alarm

攻擊

attack

危險

danger

緊急出口

emergency exit

失火了！

Fire!

滅火器

fire extinguisher

意外

accident

急救箱

first-aid kit

呼救訊號

SOS

員警

police

歐洲

Europe

北美洲

North America

南美洲

South America

非洲

Africa

亞洲

Asia

澳洲

Australia

大西洋

Atlantic

太平洋

Pacific

印度洋

Indian Ocean

南冰洋

Antarctic Ocean

北冰洋

Arctic Ocean

北極

North Pole

南極
South Pole

南極洲
Antarctica

地球
Earth

陸地
land

海
sea

島
island

國家
nation

州
state

錶盤

clock face

時針

hour hand

分針

minute hand

秒針

second hand

現在幾點？

What time is it?

天

day

時間

time

現在

now

電子錶

digital watch

分

minute

時

hour

週

week

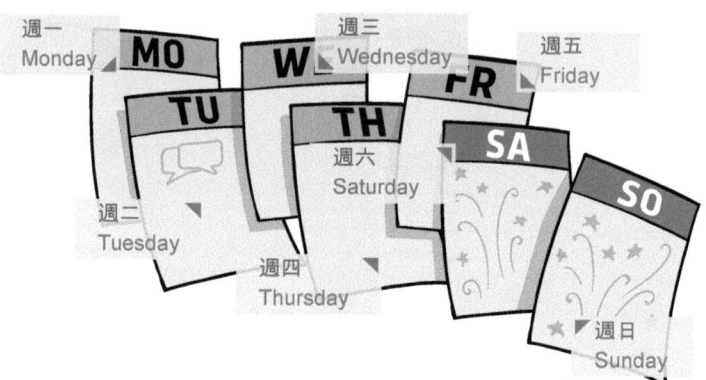

週一 Monday
週二 Tuesday
週三 Wednesday
週四 Thursday
週五 Friday
週六 Saturday
週日 Sunday

昨天

yesterday

今天

today

明天

tomorrow

早晨

morning

中午

noon

晚上

evening

工作日

business days

週末

weekend

雨
rain

彩虹
rainbow

風
wind

雪
snow

春
spring

秋
autumn

夏
summer

冬
winter

4.APRIL	11°	☀
5.APRIL	4°	☁
6.APRIL	13°	⛆
7.APRIL	8°	☀
8.APRIL	10°	☀

天氣預告

weather forecast

溫度計

thermometer

陽光

sunshine

雲

cloud

霧

fog

潮濕

humidity

閃電

lightning

打雷

thunder

風暴

storm

冰雹

hail

季風

monsoon

洪水

flood

冰

ice

一月

January

二月

February

三月

March

四月

April

五月

May

六月

June

七月

July

八月

August

九月

September

十月

October

十一月

November

十二月

December

形狀
shapes

圓形

circle

正方形

square

長方形

rectangle

三角形

triangle

球體

sphere

立方體

cube

白

white

黃

yellow

橙

orange

粉

pink

紅

red

紫

purple

藍

blue

綠

green

棕

brown

灰

grey

黑

black

很多/少許

a lot / a little

生氣/平靜

angry / calm

美/醜

beautiful / ugly

首/尾

beginning / end

大/小

big / small

明/暗

bright / dark

兄弟/姐妹

brother / sister

乾淨/骯髒

clean / dirty

完整/缺失

complete / incomplete

白天/晚上

day / night

死/生

dead / alive

寬/窄

wide / narrow

可食用/非食用

edible / inedible

邪惡/善良

evil / nice

興奮/無聊

excited / bored

胖/瘦

fat / thin

第一/最後

first / last

朋友/敵人

friend / enemy

滿/空

full / empty

硬/軟

hard / soft

重/輕

heavy / light

餓/渴

hunger / thirst

生病/健康

sick / healthy

非法/合法

illegal / legal

聰明/愚笨

intelligent / stupid

左/右

left / right

近/遠

near / far

新/舊

new / used

沒有/有些

nothing / something

老/幼

old / young

開/關

on / off

打開/闔上

open / closed

安靜/吵鬧

quiet / loud

富/窮

rich / poor

對/錯

right / wrong

粗糙/光滑

rough / smooth

傷心/高興

sad / happy

短/長

short / long

慢/快

slow / fast

濕/乾

wet / dry

溫暖/涼爽

warm / cool

戰爭/和平

war / peace

反義詞 - opposites

0

零

zero

1

一

one

2

二

two

3

三

three

4

四

four

5

五

five

6

六

six

7

七

seven

8

八

eight

9

九

nine

10

十

ten

11

十一

eleven

12

十二

twelve

13

十三

thirteen

14

十四

fourteen

15

十五

fifteen

16

十六

sixteen

17

十七

seventeen

18

十八

eighteen

19

十九

nineteen

20

二十

twenty

100

百

hundred

1.000

千

thousand

1.000.000

百萬

million

英語

English

美式英語

American English

普通話

Mandarin Chinese

印地語

Hindi

西班牙語

Spanish

法語

French

阿拉伯語

Arabic

俄語

Russian

葡萄牙語

Portuguese

孟加拉語

Bengali

德語

German

日語

Japanese

我
I

你
you

他/她/它
he / she / it

我們
we

你們
you

他們
they

誰？
who?

什麼？
what?

如何？
how?

何處？
where?

何時？
when?

名字
name

後面

behind

裡面

in

前面

in front of

上方

over

上面

on

下麵

under

旁邊

beside

中間

between

地點

place